American Indians of the Plains

of the Plains

Surviving the Great Expanse

Jennifer Prior, Ph.D.

Consultants

Katie Blomquist, M.Ed.
Fairfax County Public Schools

Nicholas Baker, Ed.D.
Supervisor of Curriculum and Instruction
Colonial School District, DE

Vanessa Ann Gunther, Ph.D.
Department of History
Chapman University

Publishing Credits

Rachelle Cracchiolo, M.S.Ed., *Publisher*
Conni Medina, M.A.Ed., *Managing Editor*
Emily R. Smith, M.A.Ed., *Series Developer*
Diana Kenney, M.A.Ed., NBCT, *Content Director*
Johnson Nguyen, *Multimedia Designer*
Lynette Ordoñez, *Editor*

Image Credits: Cover and pp. 1, 6, 25 North Wind Picture Archives; p. 2–3, 10–11 WikiArt.org/Public Domain; p. 9 (sinew) Courtesy of wanderingbull.com, (bow) Heritage Image Partnership Ltd/Alamy; p. 11 Vikas Tiwari/Dreamstime.com; pp. 12, 13, 15 Granger, NYC; pp. 14–15, 26 NativeStock/North Wind Picture Archives; p. 15 Danita Delimont/Alamy; p. 16 LOC [LC-USZ62-12277]; p. 17 (top) The Protected Art Archive/Alamy, (bottom) PARIS PIERCE/Alamy; p. 18 (top) Bettman/Getty Images, (bottom) GL Archive/Alamy; p. 19 New York Public Library Digital Collections; p. 20 Maryann Groves/North Wind Picture Archives; p. 21 (top) Wikimedia Commons/Public Domain, (bottom) JUMA Press Inc/Alamy; p. 22 LOC [DIG-ppmsca-09855]; p. 23 Lanmas/Alamy; pp. 24–25 DEA Picture Library/Getty Images; p. 27 Lee Foster/Alamy; p. 32 Wikimedia Commons/Public Domain; all other images from iStock and/or Shutterstock.

Library of Congress Cataloging-in-Publication Data

Names: Prior, Jennifer Overend, 1963- author.
Title: American Indians of the plains : surviving the great expanse / Jennifer Prior, Ph.D.
Description: Huntington Beach, CA : Teacher Created Materials, 2017. | Includes index.
Identifiers: LCCN 2015051134 | ISBN 9781493830701 (pbk.)
Subjects: LCSH: Indians of North America--Great Plains--History--Juvenile literature.
Classification: LCC E78.G73 P75 2017 | DDC 978.004/97--dc23
LC record available at http://lccn.loc.gov/2015051134

Table of Contents

People of the Plains

The Great Plains **region** spans the middle of the United States. It stretches from Canada to Mexico. And it covers the area between the Mississippi River and the Rocky Mountains. Long before this region was part of the United States, many American Indian **tribes** lived and thrived across this great expanse.

These tribes hunted buffalo. Many of them moved from place to place to follow buffalo **herds**. They gathered food from the land. They shared many religious practices and languages. Yet, each tribe was **unique**.

In the 1800s, settlers began to move west. Many moved to the Great Plains. This dramatically affected the Plains Indians. Their way of life changed forever. Still, the tribes and their **cultures** and **customs** live on.

the Great Plains

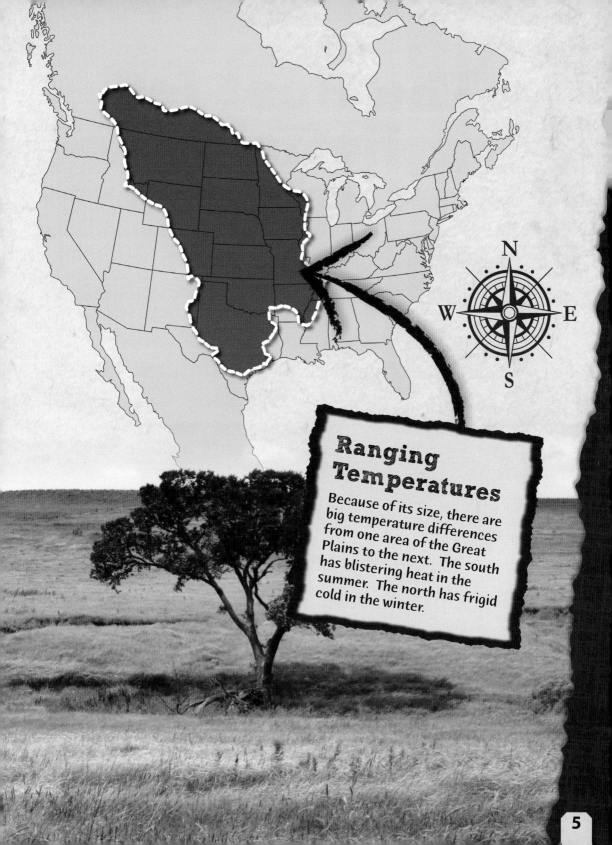

Ranging Temperatures

Because of its size, there are big temperature differences from one area of the Great Plains to the next. The south has blistering heat in the summer. The north has frigid cold in the winter.

The Hunt for Buffalo

    Life for many Plains Indians centered around the buffalo. Tribes had to be clever to hunt these very large but fast animals. Before they had horses, they tricked the buffalo. Sometimes, they ran buffalo off a cliff. Other times, a warrior wore furs to disguise himself as another animal. This drew curious buffalo out from the herd. Then, other warriors attacked it using spears and arrows. It took many people to take down a buffalo.

Bison or Buffalo?

The words *bison* and *buffalo* are often confused. Buffalo live in Africa and Asia. But they look similar to bison. When explorers saw bison, they mistakenly called them buffalo. Now, the word buffalo can be used to describe North American bison.

Asian water buffalo

bison

Because buffalo herds move from place to place, tribes had to follow them. The tribes had a **nomadic** lifestyle. They made homes that could move with them. A **tepee** made of poles and buffalo hides, or skins, made the perfect home. It gave them shelter and kept them warm. But it could be picked up and carried from place to place. This type of home helped the tribes follow buffalo herds.

tepee

The Plains Indians hunted buffalo for food. They even ate the brain, heart, kidneys, and liver. But they used the buffalo for much more than food. They used parts of the buffalo for tools and clothing and to make their homes. They used as much of the buffalo as they could.

The hide of a buffalo is very thick, so it was used to make tepees and clothing. To make the skin stronger, people tanned the hide.

tanned and painted hide

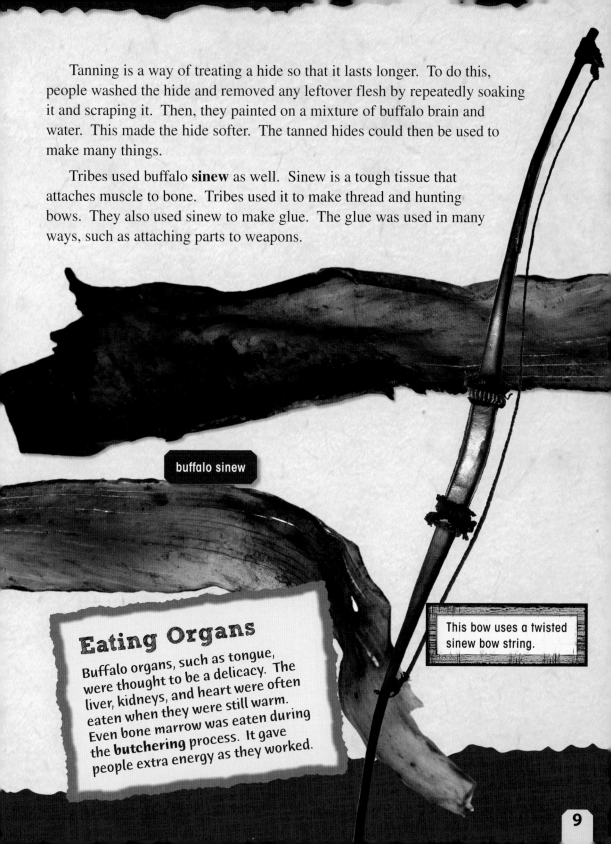

Tanning is a way of treating a hide so that it lasts longer. To do this, people washed the hide and removed any leftover flesh by repeatedly soaking it and scraping it. Then, they painted on a mixture of buffalo brain and water. This made the hide softer. The tanned hides could then be used to make many things.

Tribes used buffalo **sinew** as well. Sinew is a tough tissue that attaches muscle to bone. Tribes used it to make thread and hunting bows. They also used sinew to make glue. The glue was used in many ways, such as attaching parts to weapons.

buffalo sinew

This bow uses a twisted sinew bow string.

Eating Organs

Buffalo organs, such as tongue, were thought to be a delicacy. The liver, kidneys, and heart were often eaten when they were still warm. Even bone marrow was eaten during the **butchering** process. It gave people extra energy as they worked.

The Plains Indians even used buffalo waste! Since buffalo eat grass, their waste is basically a bundle of smelly grass. These buffalo chips, as they are called, burn easily. On the Great Plains, wood was in short supply. So tribes used buffalo chips to start fires for cooking. They used them in fires for **ceremonies** and in medicines. And tribes used stacks of chips as landmarks.

Mandan Indians perform the Buffalo Dance.

Since buffalo were used for so many things, Plains Indians were always on the lookout for them. They hoped nature would lead them to the herds. The Comanche (kuh-MAN-chee) tribe believed that horned toads would help them. A hunter would ask a horned toad where the buffalo were. They believed that the horned toad would run toward the buffalo. They also thought that a raven would circle their camp four times and then fly in the direction of a buffalo herd. Some tribes performed ceremonies to bring buffalo herds to them.

raven

horned toad

a basket of buffalo chips

Plains Cultures

Religion plays a large part in many Plains Indian cultures. The Plains Indians believe in a god known by different names. These names included Great Spirit, Big Father, and Man Above. Most believe that their god is a force that gives power to everything. They believe that every animal, plant, cloud, rock, and weather form has a spirit that came from Great Spirit. This kind of religion is called **animism**. It is the belief that everything has life and a soul.

This is a religious shrine at a Blackfoot Sun Dance house.

The Sun Dance was a ritual performed by many Plains tribes. This ceremony lasted several days. Its purpose was to ask their god for strength. They prayed the tribe would have success. During the ceremony, they danced in a circle. They did not eat or drink. Some injured themselves on purpose. They pierced their chests. They even pulled skin from their bodies. They believed their pain was a way to honor their god. Plains tribes don't do these practices today. But they have found ways to remember their old **traditions**.

Sun Dance

Art is a part of Plains culture that has survived the test of time. Plains tribes painted tepees, clothing, and horses. They even painted their bodies. The artwork of each Plains tribe was not exactly the same as the others. Many tribes used art for religious purposes. They also painted things that were important to them. So it is not surprising that many Plains paintings include buffalo.

Northern tribes made **moccasins**, baskets, and jewelry. They also wove with porcupine quills. First, they softened the quills. They used dyes made from berry juices to color the quills. Then, they wove them onto leather. Quills were used for **embroidery**, too.

painted buffalo hide

Paintings were made by many tribes to record daily life. They were like scrapbooks. Paintings of memorable events were painted on animal hides.

Many pieces of Plains artwork have been preserved, or saved. Tribal members continue to make traditional artwork.

traditional Lakota beadwork

Cheyenne painting

Floating in Space

In Plains artwork, people and animals often appear to be floating in space. They are not shown with their feet on the ground. Some say it shows that the entire world was their home. And some think it shows the spiritual world.

Plains Tribes

Plains tribes are diverse. Their cultures are as unique as the many people who dotted the Great Plains. Each tribe had its own customs and way of life.

Lakota

Like many other Plains tribes, the Lakota hunted buffalo. Their chiefs were leaders in war, medical care, and tribal rules. They also had tribal councils that helped the chiefs lead.

Lakota chief, Sitting Bull, united several tribes as the United States took over their land.

Cheyenne woman

Cheyenne

The Cheyenne did not rely on buffalo as much as other tribes. They mostly ate fish. Since they didn't move from place to place to hunt, they made permanent homes. In later years, they began to hunt more. They eventually adopted a nomadic lifestyle to follow the animals that they hunted.

Comanche chief

Comanche

The Comanche tribe broke into different groups called *bands*. While the bands were all from the same tribe, they were independent of one another. The Comanche had different practices from many of the other Plains tribes. They did not have one chief. Instead, each band of Comanche had a chief. And they didn't participate in group religious ceremonies.

Pawnee

The Pawnee Indians were hunters and farmers. They planted crops in the spring in the formation of stars. They believed this would give them a good harvest. During the summer, they left their homes to hunt. They returned in the fall to harvest. Women did much of the labor, while the grandmothers raised the children and cooked. The men were hunters and **medicine men**. Both men and women could be warriors.

Pawnee man

Osage man

Osage

The Osage (oh-SAYJ) Indians were also nomadic for part of the year. While they were away from home, the men hunted and the women butchered the animals. The women were also **foragers**. They gathered plants to eat. The men shaved their heads on the sides and wore loincloths made of deerskin that they wrapped around their hips.

Omaha

The Omaha people moved west from the Ohio River valley into the Great Plains. They adopted a nomadic lifestyle. They were hunters and farmers, too. Before they moved to the Great Plains, they made their homes out of bark. They later borrowed the idea of living in tepees from the Lakota. The men often had more than one wife. They lived in the same region as the Pawnee tribe and were protected by them.

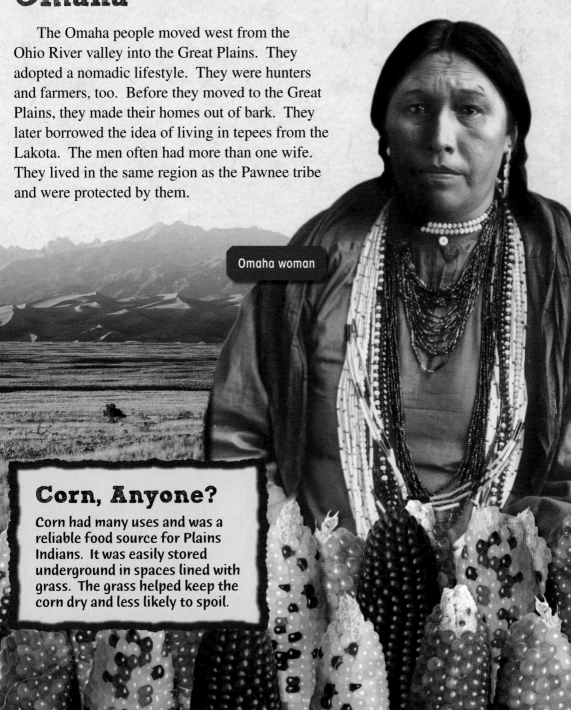

Omaha woman

Corn, Anyone?

Corn had many uses and was a reliable food source for Plains Indians. It was easily stored underground in spaces lined with grass. The grass helped keep the corn dry and less likely to spoil.

Crow

As with many of the Plains tribes, Crow men hunted. Women gathered food. Women also played important leadership roles. People listened to the advice of women and some women were chiefs. The women also set up tepees, cooked, and raised the children.

Crow chief

One Commonality

One thing all Plains tribes had in common was that their lives changed when European settlers arrived. Europeans brought horses with them. As tribes found or captured horses, their cultures began to change. They learned how to ride horses and hunt on horseback. This made hunting buffalo much easier. And it allowed tribes to travel farther. This let tribes see each other more often. Some tribes even blended into larger tribes. With horses, tribes could gather together in the summers. When they gathered, they shared stories. They held ceremonies, too.

But soon, more settlers began moving into the Great Plains. The effect was devastating for the Plains tribes.

Sign Language

When tribes met one another, it was often hard to communicate. So, they developed Plains Indian Sign Language. This silent language uses gestures instead of words. It allowed many tribes to communicate.

A student practices Plains Indian Sign Language during a powwow in 2010.

Conflict with Settlers

During the 1800s, American settlers began moving west. It was a time known as Westward Expansion. Many started to settle in the Great Plains. They moved farther and farther into tribal lands. Some tribes were kind to the settlers. Others wanted them to leave.

Manifest Destiny

During the 1800s, Americans thought that it was their destiny to move west. They imagined their country stretching from the Atlantic to the Pacific. This idea became known as Manifest Destiny.

This painting shows Americans bringing their culture westward.

Americans hunt
buffalo from a train.

As settlers in the region increased, the buffalo population decreased. Settlers killed buffalo for their hides and their meat. Some settlers killed buffalo just for the sport of it. But settlers didn't depend on buffalo the way the Plains Indians did, nor did they value them in the same way.

From 1872 to 1875, nine million buffalo were killed. This made life difficult for many Plains tribes. The animal that had supplied so many things to these tribes was disappearing. Without buffalo, many tribes did not have food. They didn't have hides for clothing and shelter. And they did not have supplies to make weapons. The Plains Indians' way of life was changed forever. And more changes were still to come.

By the 1860s, the U.S. government decided to move the tribes. They moved them to areas called **reservations**. These were small areas of land where the tribes were told to stay. They could no longer live a nomadic lifestyle. And the reservations often did not have enough food.

Many of the Plains tribes fought back. Some left the reservations. Others refused to go. Some fought American troops. Tribes won a few of the battles. They killed many U.S. troops. But with each tribal victory, more troops came. Tribes were soon outnumbered. The Plains Indians had no choice but to live on the reservations.

The life the Plains Indians had known for hundreds of years was gone. The buffalo herds had nearly been destroyed. And they had been forced to live on reservations. It was hard for the tribes to adjust to their new lives.

American troops attack the Cheyenne tribe in 1868.

Silent Killers

Settlers brought new types of diseases with them. Smallpox was one of the most contagious. Smallpox could wipe out nearly an entire village in just a few days.

People of the Plains Today

The story of these great tribes does not end in tragedy. Many of these tribes exist today. Life has changed for them, and the tribes remain strong. Reservations still exist, but people are not forced to live on them. Some choose to live there to stay connected to their tribes. They vote for leaders to make laws for them. Others keep their culture alive while living in other places. Tribal members often gather to celebrate special events and ceremonies.

Tribal members may be teachers, builders, and bankers. They are writers and storeowners. They work as farmers and professors. Their art is displayed in galleries and museums. They share their customs, beliefs, and languages. Many work to educate others about their history and traditions. They keep the history and culture of the Plains tribes alive.

This Lakota Cultural Center is on a reservation in South Dakota.

American Indians dance at a powwow in Wyoming.

Report It!

Select a topic from this book. Research your topic. You might research the lives of the Comanche people. Or you might research the many uses of buffalo. Choose a topic that interests you.

Then, use your findings to write and perform a news report about your topic. Share it with your friends. Pretend your story is breaking news. Engage your audience with an expressive voice. And be sure to make eye contact. You might even try dressing like a news anchor and recording your report!

Glossary

animism—the belief that all plants, animals, and objects have spirits

butchering—cutting meat

ceremonies—events performed because of a tradition or custom

cultures—the beliefs and ways of groups of people

customs—traditional behaviors or actions of a group of people

embroidery—the art of sewing a design

foragers—people who search for food from the land

herds—groups of animals that live together

medicine men—people in American Indian cultures who are believed to cure illnesses and keep away evil spirits

moccasins—flat shoes that are made of soft leather

nomadic—having no fixed home; moving in search of food

region—a part of an area that is different from other parts in some way

reservations—areas of land in the United States that are kept separate as places for American Indians to live

sinew—strong tissue that connects muscle to bone

tepee—a cone-shaped tent that was used by American Indians as a house

traditions—ways of thinking or doing something that has been done by a particular group for a long time

tribes—groups of people who have the same language, customs, and beliefs

unique—unlike anything else

Index

Your Turn!

Horses Come to the Americas

This painting shows an American Indian warrior riding a horse. How did horses change the lives of the American Indians of the Plains? Do you think the impact was mostly positive or mostly negative? Write a few sentences to explain your reasoning.